Great Extinctions
of the Past

D1736596

SCIENTIFIC
AMERICAN

Great Extinctions
of the Past

By Randi Mehling

An imprint of Infobase Publishing

Scientific American: Great Extinctions of the Past

Chelsea House
An imprint of Infobase Publishing
132 West 31st Street
New York NY 10001

ISBN-10: 0-7910-9049-3

ISBN-13: 978-0-7910-9049-7

Library of Congress Cataloging-in-Publication Data
Mehling, Randi.
  Great extinctions of the past / Randi Mehling.
     p. cm. — (Scientific American)
  Includes bibliographical references and index.
  ISBN 0-7910-9049-3
     1. Dinosaurs—Juvenile literature. I. Title. II. Series: Scientific American
(Chelsea House Publishers)
  QE862.D5M45 2006
  576.8'4—dc22   2006014851

Series designed by Gilda Hannah
Cover designed by Takeshi Takahashi

Printed in the United States of America

Bang GH 10 9 8 7 6 5 4 3 2 1

This book is printed on acid-free paper.

Contents

CHAPTER ONE

What Really Happened to the Dinosaurs?

There is no advance warning. Without alarms, bells, or screams, a giant **asteroid** races at 40,000 miles (64,000 kilometers) per hour toward Earth. The asteroid, the length of more than 100 football fields, crashes near the Yucatán Pennisula in northern Mexico. The explosion is far greater than if every nuclear bomb in every country on the planet exploded at the same time. The meteor leaves a hole in the ground more than 150 miles (240 km) wide. Its effects are immediate and devastating.

The heat from this smoldering **extraterrestrial** rock instantly melts sand into tiny beads of glass. The crash sets fire to plants and grinds soil and rock into powder. An immense sheet of clouds blankets the Earth, as winds carry thick dust around the planet. Earthquakes crack open the land, shoving the ocean waters in all directions. Powerful tidal waves called tsunamis flood the land with water. Volcanoes erupt, spewing hot molten lava from deep within the Earth's mantle through the cracks on the planet's surface. Millions of trees catch on fire. The lava contains sulfur and forms sulfuric acid clouds. Ashes from burned vegetation fill the air.

Within a few weeks, the sun is completely blocked, and temperatures drop on Earth by more than 20°F (11°C). Huge portions of land now lie underwater, leaving little room for land

Planet Earth is probably covered with ancient, hidden craters from asteroid and meteorite collisions, like the one illustrated here. These craters are often buried under water or land. Modern technologies, such as radar, help detect them.

animals to live. Raindrops, now made up of sulfuric acid, fall on the earth. Most of the **marine** animals and plants living in the ocean die off. They are not used to the frigid water or poisonous sulfuric acid. **Photosynthesis** stops, and plants die. On land, those that did not die from the immediate blast now have no food to eat.

A **mass extinction** has begun. When it ends, over 75% of all life on the planet will be dead. This includes every single dinosaur. The date? Sixty-five million years ago.

Since the first dinosaur fossils were found in England in 1820, scientists have been working to understand exactly what caused the dinosaurs' extinction. Was it an asteroid or several asteroids? Or did earthquakes, volcanoes, tsunamis, or sulfuric acid cause the ultimate death of the dinosaurs? This debate continues today, as scientists attempt to solve the mysteries of mass extinction.

The Age of the Dinosaurs

Most dinosaurs were amazingly powerful. Some were more than 40 feet (12 meters) long and weighed more than 35 tons. That's heavier than 20 cars.

During the history of the Earth, dinosaurs ruled the planet for a longer time than any other group of animals, including humans. Our earliest humanlike ancestors first walked the earth only about 4 million years ago. Our modern human species, *Homo sapiens*, has only been on the planet for about 195,000 years. Humans formed agricultural civilizations only about

SHOOTING STARS AND ASTEROIDS

Almost all asteroids come from part of the Main Asteroid Belt. This is the vast region of space between Mars and Jupiter. An asteroid can be made of rock, but some are made of metals like nickel and iron. Some asteroids are as small as a boulder. Others can be hundreds of miles wide. Larger asteroids occasionally crash into Earth and create craters. Craters can be found all over the world.

Asteroids often crash into each other in space. Chunks of asteroid rocks break off into smaller pieces called meteoroids. Many times meteoroids pass very close to Earth. Most of the time, they cannot survive the trip to the surface of the planet. They burn up along the way, leaving a beautiful trail of light known as a meteor, or a shooting star. If a meteoroid does land, it is known as a meteorite.

Many scientists think the Chicxulub asteroid crashed to the Earth and caused the extinction of the dinosaurs. It was named after the Mexican town near the impact site.

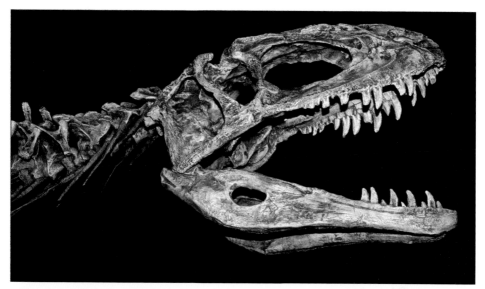

Fossils of *Tyrannosaurus rex*, one of the largest dinosaurs, are rare. Only three complete *T. rex* skulls have ever been found. Its skull was 4 feet long, and many of its 60 bone-crushing teeth were more than 10 inches long.

10,000 years ago. The United States itself has only been a nation for slightly more than 200 years. An average person's life in the United States is about 75 years.

The Age of the Dinosaurs lasted more than 150 million years. Our planet Earth was born about 4.5 *billion* years ago. It can be difficult to imagine such immense spans of time.

Fossils: Our Clues to the Past

How do scientists know what the world looked like millions of years ago? How do they know dinosaurs even existed? They learn by studying fossils, the remains of living animals and plants from the past. Fossils are preserved in certain rocks and sometimes in other materials, such as amber (hardened tree sap). Scientists called paleontologists rely on the fossil record to tell us how ancient animals and plants lived.

How does a living thing become a fossil? It can happen in several different ways. When a moist material, such as quicksand, volcanic ash, or ocean sediment, quickly buries a plant or animal, it has a good chance of becoming a fossil. Lying within these sealed tombs, hard parts, such as bones and shells, can often be found perfectly preserved, even after millions of years. Soft parts, such as hair and brains, often do not become fossils.

In other instances, the bones of a dinosaur dissolve over millions of years, but they leave an impression like a photograph in the rock. Scientists understand plant life from millions of years ago because of the impressions left by ancient leaves and sticks.

Bones can also become petrified. Bones are porous, or filled with microscopic holes. When they are quickly and tightly buried, over the years minerals gradually fill up all the holes, and the bones turn into stone. In addition, dinosaurs left huge fossilized footprints that allow scientists to trace their movements and see how they lived. Dinosaur fossils have been found all over the world.

In the late 1990s, scientists working in a desolate region of Argentina called Patagonia made a startling discovery. They found thousands of dinosaur eggs in perfect condition that had been buried by a flash flood and landslide. Using very high-tech instruments, scientists found an intact baby dinosaur inside the egg. Even the color and texture of the dinosaur skin was clearly visible. With sophisticated technology and faster computers, new species of dinosaurs continue to be discovered.

THE PUZZLING WORLD OF PALEONTOLOGY

Paleontologists use fossils to understand how, where, and when an extinct animal or plant lived. It is like putting together a jigsaw puzzle without knowing the complete picture. Paleontologists often work with zoologists. Zoologists are scientists who study living animals in order to understand how and where they live. For example, current science thinks that birds are the living relatives of dinosaurs. Paleontologists compare fossils of ancient dinosaur species with today's birds. From this, they are able to reconstruct the **evolution** and the lives of these long-dead species.

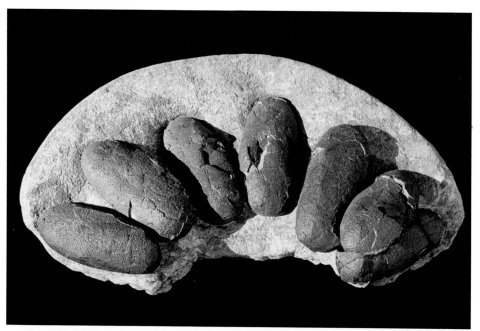

In 1924 fossilized nests and eggs were found in Mongolia. Dinosaurs were lying on top of the nests. Scientists, who thought the dinosaurs were stealing the eggs, named them *Oviraptor*, meaning "egg stealer." They later learned that the *Oviraptors* were parents, who nurtured and protected their young.

It's Hard to Become a Fossil

Only those plants and animals that had large populations, thrived on the planet for a long time, and lived in many different places all over the world stood a chance of becoming fossils. Dinosaur fossils are abundant for these very reasons. However, those fossils also needed to be well preserved to survive millions of years of erosion, the movement of streams, and the crush of thick sheets of ice called glaciers. If a burial is not airtight, bacteria often eat the entire dead body, bones and all.

Given all these conditions, it is no wonder that only 0.01% (one-tenth of one percent) of all life ever will become fossils. Of these, even fewer will actually be discovered. Even so, we still have hundreds of millions of excellently preserved fossils from as far back as 600 million years ago to help decipher the puzzles of the past.

Rocky Patterns of Life

The sediments, ash, and other materials that buried these creatures millions of years ago eventually turned into **sedimentary** rock. The fossils are found inside the rocks and sometimes in plain sight. Paleontologists conduct much patient and careful chipping away of this rock to find fossils. They create a picture of *how* these ancient animals and plants lived.

Geologists study the Earth's rocks. By analyzing ancient sedimentary rocks, these scientists tell us *when* the animals lived and when they died. Fossils and rocks are the true storytellers of Earth's history of life. Together they make up the fossil record.

Sedimentary rocks form in layers. Look at the hills and mountains. Can you see where each layer of sedimentary rock ends

Dinosaurs did not live in the Mesozoic seas, but giant marine reptiles did. These predators ruled the waters. Many had snakelike bodies, grew up to 40 feet in length, and had spiky teeth or protruding fangs.

WHAT DOES THE WORD "FOSSIL" MEAN?

The term "fossil" was first used in 1546 by a German mineralogist and scholar named Georgius Agricola in his book, *De Natura Fossilium* ("On the Nature of Fossils"). The word comes from the Latin word *fossilis*, which translates loosely as "anything dug out of the ground." The book described minerals and gemstones in addition to fossils. Agricola noted how fossils looked like living creatures but never mentioned that the fossils were the remains of actual animals or plants that were once alive. This was a subject of great debate, which was not resolved until the early eighteenth century. Agricola made important contributions to geology, mineralogy, and paleontology.

and the next layer begins? As a helpful hint, the rock layers are often different colors, shades, and textures.

The oldest layers of sedimentary rock lie on the bottom. Layer after layer piles up, one on top of the other. It can take over one million years to form just 3 feet (1 m) of sedimentary rock. Think about how many layers of rock have built up over the past 4.5 billion years!

How Fossils Tell Time

During the 1700s and early 1800s, geologists noticed an interesting pattern in sedimentary rocks. Groups of fossil animals and plants were only found in particular sections of rocks. They noticed that the fossils found in lower rocks were always older than the fossils in higher rocks. This fossil pattern repeated itself in the same **predictable** way in rocks all around the world. This was an exciting discovery. Scientists could now track the evolution of life's species.

Beginning with the oldest rocks, found on the bottom layers, the fossil record shows how the biodiversity of life keeps growing and expanding throughout the history of the planet. From the ancient past to our present, scientists have been able to date millions of species with countless shapes, sizes, and abilities.

Mass Extinction and Evolution

Because of this ability to date fossils in sedimentary rock, scientists understand that life has been successful on Earth for billions of years. Through their study of the fossil record, scientists also realize that mass extinction has always been a natural part of life's history.

A mass extinction suddenly erases most life on the planet. If large numbers of different types of animal and plant fossils are no longer found as you move from one layer of rock to another, many scientists think it is strong evidence of mass extinction—that particular species have died out. If a fossil is found in abundance, many scientists say that species was successfully thriving. These scientists believe analysis of the rocks can unlock the secrets of the past.

However, other scientists think it is a mistake to believe the fossil record as the ultimate truth of history. They think that even though a fossil is no longer found, this does not provide enough evidence to prove that a species is extinct. As we have shared earlier, there are many reasons for these types of gaps in

Paleontologists may spend more than 30,000 hours of slow and careful digging to excavate dinosaur fossils.

the fossil records. Rain, wind, glacier movements, and other natural processes can erode rocks and destroy fossils along the way. However, most scientists agree that the fossil record shows more diverse life will eventually evolve after a mass extinction, although it may take a few million years. In fact, the fossil record shows that after each mass extinction, life has become even more abundant and diverse than it was before.

The Clock of Extinction

Sedimentary rocks and the fossils they contain make up a sort of calendar called the Geologic Time Scale. This scale shows the history of life on our planet, beginning with the birth of Earth 4.5 billion years ago.

Since the 1800s, geologists have used the Geologic Time Scale to describe Earth's history. The timeline is divided into eras and periods. (An era is broken down into several shorter spans of time called periods.) For example, the dinosaurs lived during the Mesozoic Era, which began around 250 million years ago. It ended about 65 million years ago, during the Cretaceous Period, when the dinosaurs became extinct.

Geologists base these dates on the types of fossils found in the rocks. For example, dinosaur fossils first appeared in rocks that date back to 220 million years ago, during the Triassic Period. These dinosaur fossils are found in exactly the same layers of rock all over the world. Yet, in rocks dating back to 65 million years ago, there are suddenly no dinosaur fossils. Most scientists agree that this is a way of knowing dinosaurs became extinct. From observing this pattern of fossils appearing and then disappearing, it is believed that mass extinctions have happened many times since the birth of the planet.

Mass Extinctions of the World

In a mass extinction, a large number of all species vanish within in a short period of time. According to the fossil record, there have been at least ten mass extinctions throughout Earth's exis-

GEOLOGIC TIME SCALE			
ERA	**PERIOD**	**MASS EXTINCTION EVENT**	**APPROX. # YRS. AGO** (mya = millions of years ago)
Cenozoic Era (Age of Mammals) 65 mya–present	Quaternary 2 mya–present		
	Tertiary 65–2 mya		
Mesozoic Era (Age of Dinosaurs) 250–65 mya	Cretaceous 144–65 mya	Late Cretaceous mass extinction (end of Age of Dinosaurs)	─ 65 mya ─ K-T boundary mass extinction
	Jurassic 208–144 mya		
	Triassic 250–208 mya	end Triassic mass extinction	─ 208 mya
Paleozoic Era 570–250 mya	Permian 286–248 mya	end Permian mass extinction	─ 250 mya ─ P-T boundary mass extinction
	Carboniferous 360–286 mya		
	Devonian (Age of Fishes) 408–360 mya	Late Devonian mass extinction	─ 365 mya
	Silurian		
	Ordovician 505–438 mya	end Ordovician mass extinction	─ 440 mya
	Cambrian 570–505 mya		
Precambrian Era 4.5 bya–570 mya			
			─ 3.8 BILLION years ago **LIFE BEGINS IN OCEANS**
			─ 4.5 BILLION years ago **BIRTH OF EARTH**

tence. The five biggest examples were during the Ordovician Period (about 440 million years ago), the Devonian Period (about 365 million years ago), the Permian Period (about 250 million years ago), the Triassic Period (about 208 million years ago), and the Cretaceous Period (about 65 million years ago).

The most well-known mass extinction is the Cretaceous. This period described the end of the Age of the Dinosaurs. However, the biggest loss of life occurred during the Permian mass extinction. As much as 96% of all marine life died, and over 75% of all life on land died.

What Causes Mass Extinctions?

No one really knows why mass extinctions occur. There are many theories, or explanations, about their causes. Each theory has evidence to back it up.

Some scientists believe asteroids are responsible for mass extinctions. Others support theories about extraordinary volcanic eruptions or a lack of oxygen in the atmosphere. There is a common thread running through these theories: Something causes a swift, catastrophic change to the climate, making the world either very hot or very cold. These changes happen so fast that they devastate many different forms of life. Some never recover and are eventually wiped off the face of the Earth.

This book takes a deeper look at mass extinction. Read on to learn how the extinction of the dinosaurs may be the only reason we humans are here today. Be part of the scientific debate behind mass extinctions; consider the asteroid and volcano theories of mass extinction. Think about why some species survive a mass extinction while others do not. Look at the reasons behind the sixth mass extinction, happening right now. Investigate the evidence and decide what to believe for yourself.

(opposite page) Scientists created the Geologic Time Scale to tell us when different creatures lived and died throughout the history of the Earth.

CHAPTER TWO

A Brief History of the Five Biggest Mass Extinctions

bout 3.8 billion years ago, life formed in the oceans as simple soft-bodied microorganisms. There were no other types of life forms on the planet at this time. Life only existed in the oceans. For more than 3 billion years, **microorganisms** ruled the planet. Then, about 670 million years ago, a mass extinction killed nearly all life. This mass extinction is not very well known. Scientists hypothesize that a change in the ocean level could have affected the **habitat** of the microorganisms in numerous ways.

After this first mass extinction, millions of years passed. It was as though life was gathering its breath. Then, about 570 million years ago, it seemed as if a gigantic water balloon suddenly burst open. Life exploded across the world. Animals developed hard parts, like shells and skeletons. The first **vertebrates** appeared at this time. They were the earliest ancestors of all the major groups of animals, including the *human* animal. Scientists call this the Cambrian Explosion of Life.

Like a gigantic wheel, this cycle of life and extinction continues throughout the history of the Earth. Let us briefly examine the five biggest mass extinctions.

Ancestors of the sponges we harvest from the sea today first lived in the Earth's oceans about 543 million years ago. Sponges are invertebrate animals with very porous bodies that allow them to absorb lots of water.

Ordovician Mass Extinction—440 million years ago

The Ordovician mass extinction wiped out about 50% of some groups of marine animals. Some scientists think the most likely cause was an **ice age**. The Earth has experienced many ice ages over its history. An ice age is when most of the water on Earth freezes into thick sheets of ice. This would have destroyed marine habitats.

Devonian Mass Extinction—365 million years ago

The Devonian Period was known as the Age of the Fishes. The first sharks appeared, as did many kinds of primitive fishes. The Devonian mass extinction wiped out about 70% of tropical animals living in the ocean. Plants and animals on land were less affected. This mass extinction may have been caused by a global climate change, such as an ice age. This would have cooled the warm tropical waters, killing most of the animals that lived there.

The Great Dying: Permian Mass Extinction—250 million years ago

Life flourished for more than 100 million years after the Devonian mass extinction. Reptiles appeared. These were the early ancestors of the dinosaurs, yet they were not the strongest creatures on the planet. During this time, mammal-like reptiles called gorgons were the most powerful reptiles on the planet. These ferocious creatures looked half-lion and half-dragon.

Then, the largest extinction in Earth's history took place. It happened at the end of the Permian Period around 250 million years ago and lasted millions of years. It was far more devastat-

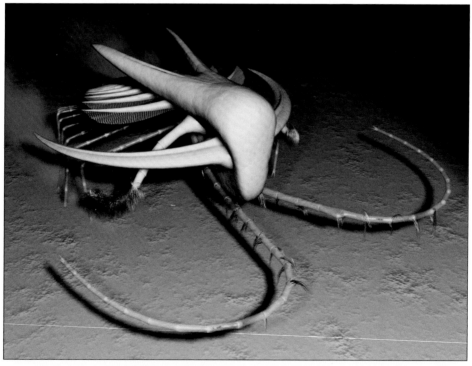

Fossils from the Canadian Rockies left records of newly evolved body shapes, such as this primitive fish from the Cambrian Period, which could be an early ancestor of crustaceans or spiders.

THE EVOLUTION OF CHARLES DARWIN'S THEORY

Charles Darwin was a British scientist in the 1800s. For five years, he sailed the oceans on the *HMS Beagle*, studying fossils, rocks, and animals from Argentina and other regions of South America. Darwin noticed that there was a resemblance between living animals and the fossils of their extinct relatives. On the Galápagos Islands off Ecuador, Darwin also found that animals such as tortoises and finches had slight var-iations in body structure and eating habits from one island to the next. He concluded that life constantly adapted to changing habitats and environments. As a result, inventive body forms evolved to fit these new environments.

Darwin published his theory of evolution in 1859 in a book called *On the Origin of Species*. It was a best seller and created huge controversy, which continues even today. Scientists all over the world have repeatedly tested Darwin's theory of evolution. The results overwhelmingly agree with Darwin. This is why the majority of the international scientific community believes Darwin's theory is fundamentally correct.

Charles Darwin became fascinated by science as a boy. His schoolmates made fun of him for his interest in chemistry and gave him the nickname "Gas."

ing than the Cretaceous mass extinction that wiped out the dinosaurs. It is estimated that as much as 96% of all marine species were lost during the Permian mass extinction. On land, more than 75% of all animals died out.

Not all land animals became extinct at this time. This is lucky for human beings. The mammal-like reptiles did not die off

During the Devonian Period, living things made their way from the sea to land for the first time in Earth's history. In this illustration, palmlike and cedarlike trees dot a lush landscape, while in the distance, smoke billows from an active volcano.

completely during this mass extinction. Scientists have theorized that mammals (including *Homo sapiens*) eventually evolved from these animals.

Some scientists believe an asteroid hit the planet and caused what is often called the Great Dying. The most recent evidence suggests that a huge volcanic explosion in Siberia may have caused massive climate change, including extreme temperatures and lack of oxygen. We will look at some of these theories in greater detail later.

Triassic Mass Extinction—208 million years ago

The Triassic mass extinction took place about 208 million years ago. About 35% of life, including the mammal-like reptiles, died at this time. Like mammals, dinosaurs evolved from the mammal-like reptiles. The Age of the Dinosaurs began in the Triassic Period, as dinosaurs began to take over the planet. True mammals appeared near the end of the Triassic. They were only as big as a shrew, with a skull several inches long. Scientists think a combination of extremely hot temperatures and a lack of oxygen were responsible for this mass extinction, similar to the causes of the Permian mass extinction.

Cretaceous (K-T) Mass Extinction—65 million years ago

Mass extinction is known by the **boundary** between one geologic time period and the next. The Cretaceous mass extinction, better known as the K-T mass extinction, happened at the boundary between the Cretaceous Period and the Tertiary Period. The K stands for Kreide, which is the German word for chalk. It describes the chalky texture of the clay found in sedimentary

An iridium layer has been found at the K-T boundary in more than 100 different places around the world.

rocks from that time. This clay layer is also known as the K-T boundary.

The Cretaceous mass extinction marked the end of the Age of the Dinosaurs. But the dinosaurs were not the only victims. Around 75% of all species were destroyed. All land animals over 55 pounds (25 kilograms) became extinct.

Some groups of animals escaped this mass extinction. There are many theories to explain why. Crocodiles, turtles, lizards, mammals, and birds were affected. However, they survived with most of their species intact. Many plants either died out or suffered heavy losses. However, the roots of many plants managed to survive and eventually grew again.

Mammals were no larger than cats at this time. Most mammals lived underground, as if waiting for their turn to dominate

Triceratops may have been the fastest dinosaur. It was able to run 22 miles per hour. The cheetah is the fastest animal today. It has been clocked at 71 miles per hour. The fastest human can run 23 miles per hour.

DINOSAURIA

In the early 1800s, the fossils of only three dinosaur species were known in Britain. The dinosaurs were considered to be huge lizards and were classified as reptiles. Sir Richard Owen was a prominent scientist and expert in anatomy (a science that studies the physical structures of living creatures) of the time. In 1841 he studied newly discovered dinosaur fossils and concluded that while the dinosaurs were related to each other, they were not related to lizards. In 1842 Sir Owen coined the name Dinosauria, from two Greek words meaning "terrible lizard," for these new members of the reptile world.

the planet. They waited about 140 million years! After the dinosaurs became extinct, the Age of Mammals began. It still took nearly 60 million *more* years for the first humanlike ancestor to walk the Earth.

The extinction of the dinosaurs has been studied extensively. For the past 25 years, most scientists have thought that a very large asteroid hit the planet. Other scientists think that a massive volcanic eruption in India caused this extinction.

Are extraterrestrial asteroids responsible for the mass extinction of the dinosaurs? Could asteroids have caused any other mass extinction? Come share in the discovery that changed the course of paleontology.

CHAPTER THREE

What Killed the Dinosaurs?

n 1977, Walter Alvarez, a young geologist, was studying rocks near Rome, Italy. He was puzzled about a particular sedimentary rock sample. There were three layers. The bottom was a thick layer of white limestone, filled with **microscopic** seashell fossils. It dated from the end of the Cretaceous Period (65 million years ago). The second was a thin layer of chalky clay. Walter did not know when or where it was from.

The third layer was red limestone. It lay on top of the other two layers. It had no fossils in it. This red rock was common in that part of Italy. It was known to be from the early Tertiary Period—the time immediately after the Cretaceous. It made sense that there were no fossils in this red rock. There were not many creatures living immediately after the Cretaceous mass extinction. But what was this mysterious clay layer? Little did Alvarez know! The rock he was holding was evidence that an asteroid may have caused the extinction of the dinosaurs.

Asteroid Evidence Rocks Paleontologists

Walter asked his father, Luis Alvarez, for his opinion on the layered rock. Luis happened to be a Nobel Prize–winning **physi-**

Fossils found in the bottom layers of sedimentary rock are older than those near the top. The oldest fossils on Earth are about 3.5 billion years old.

cist. His laboratory was testing new ways of dating rocks that contained rare **elements**.

The results were exciting and changed the paleontological world. The mysterious clay layer contained iridium. Iridium is an extremely rare element found in meteorites and asteroids from outer space.

Even better news was to come. The rock sample was 65 million years old, from the boundary between the Cretaceous and Triassic periods, also known as the K-T mass extinction. This iridium layer was found all over the world in the thin, clay layers of rocks dated to the K-T boundary. This evidence linked the time of the K-T mass extinction to these high iridium levels.

The amount of iridium in Alvarez's rock sample was measured. It was possible to estimate the size of the asteroid by knowing the amount of iridium. In 1980, the Alvarez team announced their startling news to the world. An asteroid about 6 miles (10 km) across had crashed into Earth about 65 million years ago. Was this the reason dinosaurs became extinct?

Circumstantial Evidence

The iridium seems like very convincing evidence. However, it was not enough evidence for most scientists. Scientists are careful about using **circumstantial evidence** to draw a conclusion. Just because iridium was found all over the world at the time of the Cretaceous mass extinction does not mean it is the reason for the extinction. In a court of law, just because you happen to be in the same place as the scene of a crime does not necessarily make you a suspect!

It is the same in science. It is easy for scientists to come up with the wrong answer based on only one kind of evidence. The Alvarez team needed more evidence to prove their answer was the right one.

The Evidence Is Shocking

Shocked quartz is a type of **quartz** that has peculiar telltale scratches on it. This quartz has been found near places where meteorites or asteroids are known to have crashed. Only an enormous amount of energy can scratch quartz this way. Shocked quartz has been found near nuclear bomb testing sites. As a test, scientists aimed the same amount of energy as an atomic bomb at some quartz rocks. The same patterns of scratches appeared. This proved that massive amounts of energy are required to "shock" the quartz. Rocks were analyzed from the K-T boundary in more than 30 places around the world. Each time, the results were the same. Shocked quartz was discovered in the same chalky layers of rock that contained iridium.

Scientists have found additional evidence to support the asteroid theory. An asteroid could generate enough power to produce tiny beads of glass called tektites. Scientists think that when sand is exposed to immense heat and pressure, it forms tektites. These tektites have been found in the rocks from the K-T boundary.

Dust in the Wind

Geologists think an asteroid impact would have immediately created a wall of fire. Any plants or animals within hundreds of miles would have been burned to a crisp. Soot and ash would have been the result of these fires. Very high levels of soot and ash have been found in the K-T rock layer—about 10,000 times more than normal.

Scientists also think parts of Earth's hard, rocky surface crumbled into a dustlike powder. Have you ever been in a dusty room and then opened a window? The dust flies everywhere. The same thing happened on Earth 65 million years ago. The wind blew a giant dust cloud made of iridium, ash, and soot around the world. Scientists think it eventually settled on the ground and became the clay rock layer that marks the K-T boundary.

This is more evidence that supports the asteroid theory of mass extinction.

Oil Workers Strike Gold

One of the biggest questions asked of the Alvarez team was, "Where did the asteroid actually hit the planet?" In 1981, two geologists were searching for a good place to drill for oil off the Yucatán coast of Mexico. Instead of finding oil, they discovered a crater near the town of Chicxulub (some pronounce this SHEEK-suh-loob), which became known as the Chicxulub Crater. Scientists believe the asteroid that created this crater was responsible for killing off the dinosaurs during the K-T mass extinction. They estimate that a 1-mile-wide (1.6-km) asteroid

Scientists believe that the impact of the Chicxulub asteroid caused volcanoes to erupt. Underwater volcanoes form tsunamis, which could have flooded the coasts and killed large numbers of dinosaurs.

produces a crater about 25 miles (40 km) wide. The impact of an asteroid of this size would be enough to cause massive climate changes. The crater found in Mexico was *110 to 180 miles (180–290 km)* wide! This means the asteroid that created the crater would have been about 6 miles (10 km) across. This is the same size theorized by the Alvarez team. The asteroid that formed the Chicxulub Crater was big and powerful enough to cause a catastrophe like the K-T mass extinction.

Is The Asteroid Theory the Final Word?

The Alvarez team now had a great deal of evidence to answer the question, "What killed the dinosaurs?" All over the world, high levels of iridium, tektites, shocked quartz, soot, and ash were found in rocks dating from the K-T boundary. In addition, a crater was found that matched the size of an asteroid large enough to cause a mass extinction. These findings support an asteroid theory of mass extinction.

New evidence suggests that more than one asteroid hit the planet around 65 million years ago. Several large craters have been found. The Silverpit Crater was found in the United Kingdom, the Boltysh Crater in Ukraine, and the Shiva Crater off the coast of India. These craters are all about the same age as the Chicxulub Crater. This recent evidence increases the support of

Flying reptiles known as *Pterosaurs* had wingspans ranging from a few inches to 36 feet. Their wings were covered with a leathery membrane that stretched between the body, the top of the legs, and an elongated fourth finger. Claws protruded from the other fingers.

the asteroid theory. The size of the Shiva Crater suggests that a 25-mile-wide (40-km) asteroid formed it. This is four times the size of the asteroid that hit Mexico! The destructive force of all these asteroids combined may have finally killed off the mighty dinosaurs.

The Dinosaur Debates Continue

Today, many scientists believe the asteroid theory is the best explanation for the end of the dinosaurs. However, this is still the subject of scientific debate. For example, some scientists argue that the dinosaurs had been dying off for millions of years before the asteroid(s) hit Earth. If they were already a dying race, then an asteroid crash may have been the final straw, but not the only reason, for their extinction.

The scientific process is never over. New evidence is constantly being discovered to challenge older theories. New perspectives on older theories also provide lively debate in scientific conferences and literature. These debates force scientists to prove a hypothesis with predictable, repeatable results in order to be taken seriously. Recently, scientists discovered other sedimentary rocks that contain tektites, shocked quartz, and iridium. These rocks date back millions of years, *but do not match up with any times of mass extinction.* This throws a shadow of doubt on the asteroid theory of dinosaur extinction, but before we can really decide if this evidence is worthy, it needs to undergo further scientific scrutiny and testing.

In Darwin's age, scientists used pencil and paper to figure out long mathematical equations. Today, we have sophisticated computers that can calculate in five minutes what it took Darwin's contemporaries years to do. Computers and other advanced technology allow today's scientists to delve even deeper into the mysteries of the fossil record, and to learn more about life's evolution each year. To prove this point, in the past five years, scientists have uncovered new evidence that shows how volcanic eruptions can also create high iridium levels in sedimentary rock. Will this evidence prove that volcanoes, not asteroids, actually caused the K-T mass extinction? Read on to the next chapter to uncover the evidence.

CHAPTER FOUR

Volcanoes and the Great Permian Mass Extinction

As much as 96% of life died during the Permian mass extinction, the Great Dying. This was the biggest mass extinction in the history of the planet. It occurred many millions of years before the dinosaurs ever existed. What could have caused this mass extinction of life on Earth?

For many years, the scientific community has believed that an asteroid was responsible for the Permian mass extinction. They thought the same force that killed off the dinosaurs also caused the Permian mass extinction. The time of the Great Dying is also known as the P-T mass extinction since it happened at the boundary between the Permian and Triassic periods. High iridium levels were found in the rock layers dated to the P-T mass extinction—just like those found at the K-T boundary. This has been a main piece of evidence to support the asteroid theory for both mass extinctions.

Several years ago, scientists made another fascinating discovery. They were searching in China, Japan, and Hungary for clues and patterns in rocks from the P-T boundary. They found small

Volcanic eruptions are fairly common and still change the face of the Earth today. It is estimated that approximately 600 of the world's volcanoes are currently active.

bubbles of air trapped in the rocks. This was the same air breathed by animals about 250 million years ago! It contained high levels of two very rare gases called helium and argon. The exact amounts of helium and argon found in these rocks are known to exist only in asteroids and meteorites. Scientists think this discovery adds more supporting evidence for the asteroid theory.

Volcanoes Challenge Asteroid Theory

However, in the past two or three years, exciting new evidence has challenged the asteroid theory for both the K-T *and* the Permian mass extinctions. High levels of iridium were found in the hot molten lava that erupts from enormous volcanoes. This evidence has been dated. It seems that several volcanic eruptions happened about 248 million years ago and about 63 million years ago. This links volcanic eruptions to both the Cretaceous and Permian mass extinctions. Why is iridium found in lava?

Iridium in Mantle Plumes

The Earth is made up of layers. The crust of the Earth is its outside layer. The core of the Earth is the deepest part inside the planet. The mantle lies in between these two parts. Recent research has shown that the Earth's mantle contains high levels of iridium.

As the mantle heats up, it melts and explodes through the Earth's surface in the form of a huge volcanic eruption. This explosion is known as a **mantle plume**. The melted mantle is called lava when it oozes through cracks in the Earth's surface, bringing iridium along with it. Therefore, volcanic eruption can explain the high levels of iridium in sedimentary rock. This same evidence—iridium—can now "prove" *both* asteroids and volcanoes as the causes of mass extinction.

After the volcano stops erupting, the lava eventually cools. The cooling lava forms a type of volcanic rock called basalt. Basalt is very easy to identify. It has a special texture and other unique qualities. The cooling lava also creates formations that often look like stacked pancakes.

GORGONS RULE

It was a fearsome animal, with a lion-shaped head and a body of a reptile. Its huge head had large lizard eyes and was covered in reptilian scales and may have had tufts of fur. This carnivore (meat eater) was more than twice as large as an average human man. Saberlike teeth protruded from its mouth, ready to tear apart its next meal. Large claws extended from its large flat feet. A long scaly tail whipped about behind it. Like a wolf, it loped after its prey, never stopping until it made its kill. This is a gorgon. Gorgons ruled during the Permian Period about 260 million years ago. The first dinosaurs appeared about 30 million years later and eventually took control of the planet from the gorgons. A gorgon is considered a mammal-like reptile—and it is your mammalian ancestor from millions of years ago. It is the ancestor of the dinosaurs as well.

The Proof Is in the Pancakes

Basalt pancake formations exist in both Siberia and in India. They are called the Siberian Traps in Siberia and the Deccan Traps in India. Scientists have linked the date of the K-T mass extinction to the date of the Deccan volcano explosion. They drilled deep into the sedimentary rocks on the ocean floor near India. The fossil samples they found showed that the Deccan Traps were formed during the end of the Cretaceous Period. This connects an active volcano with the time of mass extinction. Similar evidence shows many other massive volcanoes erupted about 65 million years ago.

Analysis of the volcanic basalt rocks of the Siberian Traps paints a similar picture. They have been dated from the time of the Permian mass extinction.

Some scientists theorize that these volcanoes erupted continuously for several million years. The lava flooded the Earth and

THE DINOSAUR–BIRD CONNECTION

There were very low levels of oxygen in the air during the Permian and Triassic mass extinctions. Scientists think that many life forms actually suffocated. However, reptiles did not die. They adapted to the low oxygen in the air and survived both mass extinctions. By the middle of the Triassic Period, they evolved into dinosaurs.

For many years, scientists wondered if modern birds were related to ancient flying dinosaurs. Today most scientists agree that fossils show us how birds evolved from dinosaurs. In 2003 scientists discovered more evidence of the dinosaur-bird connection. They found that the lungs of today's birds are the same as the lungs of yesterday's dinosaurs. To many scientists, it makes sense. Dinosaurs evolved during times of low oxygen. We know that birds do not require as much oxygen to breathe as humans and other mammals do. They can fly over mountains that are 30,000 feet (9,000 m) high. There is very little breathable oxygen at that altitude. As birds evolved from dinosaurs, they inherited the ability to make do with less oxygen.

Giant basalt columns were formed by continuous, full-intensity volcanic eruptions that lasted about one million years. The Siberian Traps basalt formation is larger than all of Europe.

buried vast stretches of land and sea. This could help explain the high levels of iridium found all over the world in rocks dated from both mass extinctions.

In addition, these scientists suggest that the scratch patterns on shocked quartz could be from volcanic explosions, not asteroid impacts. The date of the volcanic rocks, the high levels of iridium, the soot and ash, and the shocked quartz provide much evidence to support the volcano theory.

Asteroids or Volcanoes—Was It Both?

Most of the scientific community still favors the asteroid theory as the cause of the K-T mass extinction. However, some scientists wonder if a volcanic eruption caused the beginning of the

Iguanodans were one of the most widespread dinosaurs. Their fossils have been found in many regions of the world, including Europe and North America. Evidence points to their having lived in large herds.

dinosaur destruction. They think an asteroid crash (or crashes) happened after an eruption and eventually finished off the dinosaurs.

A growing number of scientists can show evidence that the Permian mass extinction was caused by a combination of both asteroids and volcanoes. These scientists think that the world of the dinosaurs became very cold. They think the Permian world became unbearably hot and dry. Also, research suggests that it became very difficult to breathe at the time of the P-T mass extinction. The amount of oxygen in the air dropped to half of what we find in the atmosphere today. In fact, today some scientists believe the majority of life suffocated from a combination of extremely high temperatures and a severe drop in breathable oxygen.

Extreme Heat and Suffocation

This recent view sees the Permian mass extinction as a *series of extinctions*. Each extinction set off another one in a **chain reaction**. The massive volcanic eruptions in Siberia may have been the first part of this Permian chain reaction. These eruptions may have increased the world's temperature by releasing huge amounts of heat and molten lava. The volcano also released thick clouds of **carbon dioxide**. Carbon dioxide acts like a blanket that traps warm air on the surface of the planet. As temperatures soared, life began to die off in great numbers.

Marine plankton are tiny plants that live in the ocean. Scientists believe that marine plankton produce most of the breathable oxygen on the planet. Fossil records show that over 99% of all marine plankton died during the Permian mass extinction. This might explain the big drop in oxygen levels at the time. However, there were even more reasons oxygen levels went down.

Methane is a gas that is usually frozen in the coldest places on Earth. Scientists think the frozen methane melted like an ice cube in the Sun. This released the methane gas into the air. Methane sucks oxygen out of the air and transforms itself into

PHEW! DID ROTTEN EGGS HELP KILL PERMIAN LIFE?

Bacteria living on the bottom of the ocean produce a stinky gas called hydrogen sulfide. It smells like rotten eggs. It is also very poisonous. Scientists think this toxic gas killed a lot of life both on land and in the oceans. Currently, scientists are searching for fossilized green sulfur bacteria as evidence to prove this part of the theory behind the great Permian mass extinction.

carbon dioxide. Now the world got even hotter as more carbon dioxide trapped more warm air. It probably became even harder to breathe, as the oxygen levels in the air went down even further. Scientists think a lot of life's creatures may have suffocated without enough oxygen in the air.

This chain reaction of extinction continued. The surface of the Earth became hotter and hotter. Scientists estimate the temperature may have increased over 40°F (23°C). They think this combination of extreme heat, suffocation, or a mixture of both wiped out over 96% of all life during the Great Dying period around 250 million years ago. First, most life in the world's oceans became extinct. Life on land followed soon after. The entire Permian mass extinction lasted several million years.

CHAPTER FIVE

Surviving Mass Extinction

You might not be here, reading this book, if the dinosaurs had not become extinct. Why did mammals survive and dinosaurs perish at the end of the Cretaceous Period? Many of life's creatures cannot adapt quickly enough to catastrophic changes. The result is mass extinction. However, there are always some survivors. Is it possible to predict who might survive and who might perish from a catastrophic change to the environment?

Most animals and plants live in very specific climates and geographic locations. Life adapts to changing living conditions very slowly and gradually, over millions of years. Those animals and plants most able to adapt often evolve into new species. A species might evolve into a new body shape or gain a new body part or function, such as claws for climbing trees or the ability to see in the dark. If these new species are better adapted to their new environments, they flourish. Animals and plants that are unable to adapt to changing conditions die off. They become extinct.

During mass extinction, there is usually a sudden and severe change in the weather. In a sense, the world gets extremely

More than 90% of all turtle species survived the K-T mass extinction. Today more than half the world's turtles face extinction.

stressed out. There is no time to get used to different temperatures. There is no time to **adapt** to a new environment. In these situations, animals and plants have two choices. They can find new homes that suit them better or they can stay and try to make the best of their new living conditions. In both scenarios, if they can't cope, they die off. Adapt or perish is the name of this evolutionary game. Charles Darwin called it natural selection.

Mass Extinction = Evolution
During ordinary times, it is natural for some species to die off and become extinct. After they die, their homes, called **ecological niches**, become vacant. Species have a natural tendency to spread out and quickly take over any vacant ecological niches. Then they slowly adapt to their new homes. Fossil records show how living creatures grow new body parts or change a particular behavior in order to fit into their new environment. This adaptation usually takes place over thousands of years, and species

TRICERATOPS

The *Triceratops* traveled in enormous herds, like today's elephants do. The largest adults formed the outside of the herd. They protected their young by surrounding them. These parenting abilities show that some dinosaurs formed strong social communities. This may help explain why dinosaurs survived and thrived for 150 million years.

become more diverse over this long period of time. Those species that do not adapt eventually perish.

However, after a mass extinction, millions of ecological niches are suddenly left empty. The survivors of mass extinction rapidly begin to fill these empty niches. This allows many more species to adapt to new environments than under normal circumstances. Scientists think this is the reason behind the huge explosion of life's diversity after extinction. Life quickly evolves to fill every single empty nook and cranny of the world.

Billions of species have lived and died since life began on Earth. Fossil records show that a species never repeats itself.

Fossilized human skeletons were discovered in caves in southern France. Dating of the fossils tells us that prehistoric humans lived there about 2 million years ago in the Late Tertiary Period.

Think of the **biodiversity** the world has witnessed! It is estimated that there are 10 million different species alive today.

Survival of the Fittest

Many times, several species will try to move into an empty niche at the same time. There is only so much food and space to go around. Species constantly compete with each other for space and resources. Only the most adaptable species will win out and get to stay in this new home. If a species cannot adapt to another habitat, it becomes extinct. This is known as survival of the fittest. Along with natural selection, it is another important part of the theory of evolution.

A species that becomes extinct is not necessarily weak. Look at the dinosaurs. They were the strongest creatures on Earth for over 150 million years. Tiny ratlike mammals survived, while

Alligators are reptiles and are closely related to dinosaurs. Thanks to conservation laws, the American alligator is at low risk for extinction. Once her eggs hatch, a mother alligator carries between 8 and 10 babies in her mouth to the water and then opens her jaws to encourage the babies to swim out.

not a single dinosaur was alive by the end of the Cretaceous Period. Crocodiles, insects, and frogs survived. Plant roots survived. Which special characteristics allow some to survive while others die off?

Does Size Matter?

This is another subject of great scientific debate. Some scientists say size matters. An investigation of extinction evidence shows that larger animals tended to become extinct more often than smaller animals. This could be related to the fact that larger animals tend to have smaller populations and do not have as many offspring. Larger animals also tend to live in small geographical areas. These facts would seem to make larger animals more susceptible to extinction. A species is more likely to survive if it reproduces quickly, has a large population, and is spread out all over the world.

However, there is much evidence that can be used to prove the opposite of this argument. Let us take the dinosaurs as an example. Every dinosaur died off, leaving mammals to survive. It is true that mammals were often no bigger than a shrew. However, several dinosaur species were also no bigger than the average mammal. Additionally, dinosaurs lived in every ecological niche available on the planet. Some species laid thousands of eggs each year. To this day, scientists have still not been able to prove that larger animals are more likely to become extinct than smaller animals.

Survival or Extinction—Plain Ole Luck?

Currently, many scientists think survival is a combination of a great deal of adaptability and a healthy dose of plain ole good luck.

Natural selection happens very slowly and gradually. This means only a few species die out every million years or so. Even

CASE STUDY: COLD BLOODED VERSUS WARM BLOODED

Some scientists have wondered if body temperature has anything to do with surviving the K-T mass extinction. Reptiles like crocodiles and alligators are **cold-blooded** animals. They need direct sunlight shining on them to stay warm. If it is cold and rainy, their bodies become very cold. Mammals are **warm-blooded** animals. Their bodies stay warm whether it is sunny outside or not. For example, humans maintain a constant body temperature of 98.6°F (37°C). Warm-blooded animals need to eat all the time to maintain their body temperature.

During the K-T mass extinction, we are sure of one thing: The temperature changed in extreme ways. We do not know if the world became extremely hot or extremely cold. Perhaps the warm-blooded mammals adapted more easily to these shifts in temperature. Scientists theorize this could be one of the reasons mammals survived.

However, cold-blooded animals survived as well—crocodiles, turtles, alligators, and lizards, to name a few. Some say cold-blooded animals had an advantage. They could slow their bodily processes down and not eat for long time spans. This allowed them to wait out the disaster until the temperatures went back to normal.

Both cold-blooded reptiles and warm-blooded mammals survived the K-T mass extinction. Research suggests that some dinosaur species were warm blooded and others were cold blooded. However, there were no surviving dinosaurs. At this point, scientists cannot say if survival is linked to body temperature.

The great auk was a flightless bird last seen around 1844. Several factors predicted its extinction: it did not breed until it was several years old, laid only a few eggs at a time, and did not have many safe places to raise its young. Still, humans, who killed thousands of auks for their feathers, oil, and meat, are the main reason for their extinction.

so, after intense investigations of the evidence over many years, it seems that no one can predict exactly what will make one species more adaptable than another. The very traits that will allow one species to adapt and survive are unknown. These specialized survival traits only emerge when a species is confronted by a new situation. We have all heard heroic stories about people finding incredible strength, for example, to pull a car off another person. This shows us how we never really know what hidden strengths we have until we need them.

As we have seen, these rules of survival—adapt or die—are doubly true during a mass extinction. Most species cannot adapt quickly enough in these extreme circumstances and die off. Yet, a few do survive even these most challenging circumstances. If a species' size does not matter, what traits help some survive while others become extinct?

Random luck. Fossil records show that the very traits that helped species adapt and survive during ordinary times have *nothing* to do with living through a mass extinction. In fact, scientists **hypothesize** that those exact same traits could even be *the cause* of their extinction. Those species that do endure a mass extinction just happen to have some surprising special trait that allows them to survive. Therefore, many evolutionary scientists conclude that it is impossible to predict exactly who will outlive a mass extinction.

To sum it up, life is unpredictable. Who would have bet that dinosaurs would become extinct and mammals would thrive? Either way, perhaps humans should just thank their lucky stars it turned out this way!

CHAPTER SIX

Are We Headed for the Next Mass Extinction?

Right now, we may be in the middle of a mass extinction that could be bigger than the one that killed off the dinosaurs.

Like all life, humans are a species on an endless path of evolution. If there is an empty space on the planet, we rush to fill it. Today, humans live in every corner of the globe. We are not the most numerous species. There are millions more insects than there are humans. We are not the oldest species. Cockroaches have roamed the planet for much longer than we have. Every species adapts *to* its environment. Yet humans have an increasing ability to change the environment so that the environment is better adapted to *them*.

Humans are the only species that has flown to the Moon or created a computer microchip. Humans also are the only species that overhunts, pollutes, and destroys vast miles of habitat. This is a unique combination of traits! Will these traits be the keys to our survival as a species? Or will these traits be our undoing? For the first time in life's 3.8 billion–year history, our species—humans—can alter the Earth as no other life form has ever done

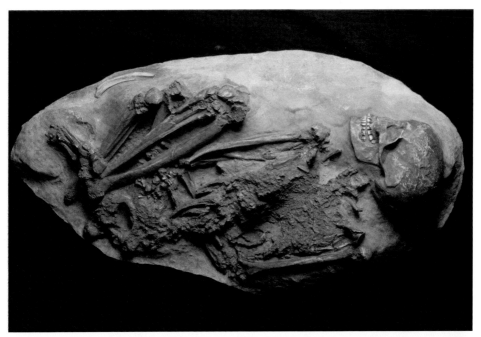

A fossilized Cro-Magnon skeleton is only partially uncovered from its rocky grave. It lay undisturbed for about 40,000 years before paleontologists unearthed it.

before. Let us look more deeply into the potential causes behind this modern mass extinction.

The Ice Age and the First Extinction Caused by Humans

About 195,000 years ago, the modern human species appeared. Humans shared food, living space, and diseases with every other animal, plant, and bacteria. The small number of people who lived back then did not have advanced weapons. They were both **predator** and **prey**, just like all other living species. Sometimes humans killed for food. Sometimes others ate them. For thousands of years, humans lived in this balanced relationship with nature.

During the most recent ice age, thick sheets of ice covered the planet. Temperatures were about 25°F (13°C) colder than a typical winter day today. Many species could not deal with the cold weather. They either moved to warmer places or died.

The human species proved to be very adaptable. Archaeologists are scientists who study ancient human civilizations. They think humans developed sharp-pointed weapons and new hunting techniques sometime during the Ice Age. During this time, many **mammals** known as **megafauna** grew to enormous sizes. Wooly mammoths looked like hairy elephants and were as tall and heavy as two cars. Mastodons, giant beavers, saber-toothed cats, and teratorn birds with 25-foot (8-m) wingspans also lived along the edges of the ice sheets.

Around 10,000 years ago, the ice melted. *Homo sapiens* explored and settled new lands previously covered under ice. (Today, ice sheets only remain over Antarctica and Greenland.) They formed

Mastodons, mammoths, horses, camels, bison, a sloth, and a great blue heron join Paleo-Indians in this scene from 33,000 years ago. Fossil remains found in northwest Oklahoma offer the earliest evidence we have of human life in North America.

the first farming communities. Some say human civilization began at this time. Humans used their new hunting skills and hunted the megafauna into extinction. It was the first extinction caused by human beings. Unfortunately, it was not the last.

Warp-Speed Extinction

Throughout life's history, there has always been a low level of extinction. This is called **background extinction**. It is like low music playing while you do your homework. As species die off, new species evolve a bit faster. The fossil record shows how the diversity of life has always increased.

Mass extinction is very different from background extinction. It is like a sudden, startling blare of music. Many species suddenly die, and new species do not evolve fast enough to take their place. Today, species are dying off at warp speeds—1,000 to 10,000 times the speed of background extinction. As in times of mass extinction, evolution is having trouble keeping up. The biodiversity on the planet is decreasing at an alarming pace. At the current rate, scientists predict that one out of every five animals and plants on the Earth will become extinct within the next 25 years! Some say this is a low number, and project that nearly half of all life on the planet will become extinct during this short amount of time.

The greatest threat to the world's living creatures is the destruc-

FOSSIL FUELS

Coal, oil, and gas are called "fossil fuels" because they have been formed from the fossilized remains of prehistoric plants and animals. They provide about 95% of the world's energy for such needs as heating, transportation, electricity, and more. Fossil fuels are not a renewable energy source. Once they are gone, they are gone forever. You could argue that fossil fuels are renewable because life on the planet will eventually die and become fossils. However, it took millions of years for fossils to become fuel.

Mammoths became extinct about 11,000 years ago. Many scientists specu-
late that early humans hunted these ancestors of our modern elephant into
extinction, but climate change or disease may also have contributed to
their demise.

tion of their habitats. Natural habitats all around the world are
cut down or paved over as the human population expands. For
example, over half of every animal and plant species in the *entire
world* live in the warm tropical forests in Australia, Asia, Africa,
Mexico, and South America. Each year the Earth's forests shrink

Are We Headed for the Next Mass Extinction? 57

What do pandas, monkeys, and frogs have in common? Habitat destruction. People are kicking them out of their homes! People are building more cities and taking over natural spaces, such as rain forests and wetlands. As animals lose their homes and their food supply, their survival is at stake.

by more than 40 million acres.

In addition, human populations create more waste than the Earth can absorb. The result is pollution. Poisonous chemicals have polluted our air and water, killing numerous species of wildlife either directly or by devastating their habitats. The cycle of evolution does not stop. The choices are to adapt or perish. Many species have or will become extinct.

Ecosystems and the Web of Life

Forests, streams, deserts, and oceans are examples of ecosystems. An **ecosystem** is the relationship between living creatures and the places they live. For example, some plants, insects, and birds live in the cool pine forests of Maine. Other species live in the desert in southern Arizona. One frog might live in trees while another lives its whole life under a rotting log. Earth is home to an incredibly diverse community of life, with a huge variety of ecosystems. Few of these species would survive by switching homes with another.

Healthy ecosystems provide the world with clean air and water. They also provide us with food, medicine, and shelter. Ecosystems need lots of diversity to do these important jobs. For example, humans depend upon agricultural crops such as wheat to make bread. The crops need water and soil to grow. Healthy soil is alive with microorganisms, bugs, and worms. Soil feeds the plants that eventually feed the humans. The plants also produce oxygen so all life's creatures can breathe. Worms eat the microorganisms. Birds eat the worms. Bird droppings fertilize the soil with microorganisms. There are many more interconnections even in this simple example.

Upsetting the Apple Cart

What might happen if all the worms died? How many other members of the ecosystem would be affected? How would humans be affected?

Out of the approximately 10 million species alive today, we only know 1.4 million of them. If scientists are correct, about 2 million species will become extinct within the next 25 years. We can already see the health of the world's ecosystems decline as

ENDANGERED

Across the world, more than 6,000 animal species are listed as endangered. Polar bears, elephants, whales, gorillas, tigers, and pandas are a mere few from that list.

As of 1990, the tropical rain forest was shrinking over 40 million acres per year. This is about the size of the state of Washington. At this rate, within 75 years all the rain forests could be gone, along with millions of species that make the rain forest their home.

The bald eagle is the national symbol of the United States. It is one of the largest flying birds, with an 8-foot (2.4-m) wingspan—as long as a big dining room table. This powerful species has adapted several special characteristics that make it very good at surviving. For instance, it can see four to eight times farther than humans. Bald eagles also have razor-sharp talons that help them hold fish during flight. The most impressive feature of this bird is its curved beak, used to tear fish apart while eating.

Because of human pollution, this mighty creature was close to extinction. The culprit was a chemical called DDT, used by farmers as an insecticide. DDT got into the water supply and contaminated fish, which is the main food source of the bald eagle. DDT affected the eggs they produced so there were very few baby eaglets born. This caused a huge decrease in the eagle population. DDT is now illegal in the US, and there are other laws protecting these majestic birds. Because of these efforts, the bald eagle is no longer an endangered species.

Historians say large numbers of bald eagles soared overhead during the War of Independence against the British. This majestic bird soon became our national symbol. Over the next 200 years, thousands of eagles were killed by hunters and due to the effects of DDT. They are now a protected species, and their numbers are on the rise.

the number of species decreases. We do not even know what most of those species are! What if one of those extinct plant species is a plant that could cure cancer? We will never know, because once a species is extinct, it is gone forever.

Eventually, new species will evolve and biodiversity will increase. However, the same species never repeats itself. And the wait to see these new species will be very long. Recent scientific studies show that it takes about 10 million years for biodiversity to increase after any type of extinction, whether it is a background or mass extinction. To put that amount of time in perspective, our earliest human ancestors are only about 4 million years old.

Saving the World's Ecosystems

For the first time in life's history, the human species has the power to cause mass extinction. We are also perhaps the first species that can prevent it. There are many laws that protect the habitats of species in danger of becoming extinct. Countries around the world are setting aside vast sections of land and ocean just for wildlife. There are hundreds of organizations, such as the World Wildlife Federation, The Nature Conservancy, and Conservation International, whose sole purpose is to protect ecosystems from human destruction.

As of 2003, there were more than 100,000 protected wildlife areas around the world. These include parks, wildlife refuges, and other reserves, both on land and in the ocean. They cover about 12% of the Earth's surface. Protected areas cover over 16% of Southeast Asia alone. This is a large increase from 10 years ago, when protected areas covered only 3% of the world.

Hopefully, conservation efforts like these can offset the destructive effects of other human activities. Whatever the outcome, we can be certain of one thing: the Earth and its inhabitants will continue to evolve in fascinating and unpredictable ways.

Glossary

adapt – to become used to a new environment or different conditions

asteroid – an irregularly shaped rock that orbits the Sun, mostly in a band called the asteroid belt between Mars and Jupiter

background extinction – the normal pattern of species death as life evolves and either dies or adapts to changing environmental conditions. Slightly more new species evolve to take over the spaces left behind by extinct species.

biodiversity – the variety of life that lives in a particular place

boundary – the point at which something ends and something new begins

carbon dioxide – a colorless, odorless gas produced after breathing and used by plants as food during photosynthesis. It is also caused by combustion, such as volcanic eruptions.

chain reaction – a series of events following one after another, each of which causes the next one to happen

circumstantial evidence – facts that are related to a circumstance but cannot be connected to a definite cause

cold-blooded animal – an animal with internal body temperature that varies according to the temperature of its surrounding environment

ecological niche – a particular place where an organism lives

ecosystem – a group of living organisms in a particular environment dependent upon each other and the special conditions of that environment

element – a substance that cannot be broken down into a simpler one by a chemical reaction

evolution – the process of natural selection, survival of the fittest, and luck where life develops from simple to complex organisms

extraterrestrial – from outer space

habitat – the natural home of a living organism, such as a forest or desert

hypothesize – to make an educated guess

ice age – a reoccurring time when most of the Earth is covered in thick ice sheets, and the temperature is very cold. An ice age can last millions of years. The last ice age ended about 15,000 years ago. Since there are still glaciers and ice sheets, we are considered to be in a warm, interglacial period at the present time.

mammal – a warm-blooded vertebrate that gives birth to live young

mantle plume – an enormous volcanic eruption

marine organism – an organism that lives in the sea or ocean

mass extinction – the death of over 50% of all life on Earth within a short geological time

megafauna – very large animals

methane – A colorless, odorless, flammable gas that is the main part of natural gas. Natural gas is used as fuel.

microorganism – an organism that is so small you need a microscope to see it

microscopic – invisible to the naked eye, can only be seen with a microscope

photosynthesis – The process by which green plants use the energy of the sun and carbon dioxide to produce their own food and create oxygen as a byproduct

physicist – a scientist who studies the relationship of matter, energy, force, and motion

population – the number of individuals of a plant or animal species

predator – an animal that hunts, kills, and eats other animals to survive

predictable – the ability to say what is going to happen in the future based on past experience

prey – animals that are caught, killed, and eaten by other animals as food

quartz – a crystalline mineral found in rocks

sedimentary – a type of rock formed as dirt, dust, and dead organisms compress over time into hard layers

species – a group of living creatures that share unique similarities to each other. Individuals from different species usually cannot produce off-spring together. Humans are part of a species called *Homo sapiens*. If an entire species dies out, it is considered extinct.

terrestrial – belonging to the land rather than the sea or air

vertebrate – an animal that has a backbone

warm-blooded animal – an animal with internal body temperature that is constant, and does not depend on the temperature of its surrounding environment

Bibliography

Bakker, Robert T., Ph.D. *The Dinosaur Heresies*. New York: Zebra Books, 1986.

Basu, Asish, and Paul R. Renne. "Massive Volcanic Eruptions in Siberia Links to Largest Extinction." www.rochester.edu/pr/releases/ear/basu2.htm.

Benton, Michael. "Accuracy of Fossils and Dating Methods." www.actionbio science.org/evolution/benton.html.

Boulter, Michael. *Evolution and the End of Man*. New York: Columbia University Press, 2002.

Cardiff University. "Is This What Killed the Dinosaurs? New Evidence Supports Volcanic Eruption Theory." www.sciencedaily.com/releases/2003/09/030915 074538.htm.

Chiappe, Luis M., and Lowell Dingus. *Walking on Eggs*. New York: Simon & Schuster, 2001.

Gould, Stephen Jay. *Wonderful Life—The Burgess Shale and the Nature of History*. New York: W. W. Norton & Company, 1989.

Joseph, Lawrence E. *Gaia—The Growth of an Idea*. New York: St. Martin's Press, 1990.

Larsen, Janet. "Eco-Economy Updates. The Sixth Great Extinction: A Status Report." Earth Policy Institute. www.earth-policy.org/Updates/Update35.htm.

Mirsky, Steve. "I Shall Return." *Earth*. April 1998.

NewScientist.com. "Mass Extinction Theory on the Rocks." *New Scientist*. Issue 2509, p. 17. www.newscientist.com/article.ns?id=mg18725095.000.

Paine, Michael. "Asteroid/Comet Impact Craters and Mass Extinctions and Shiva Hypothesis of Periodic Mass Extinctions." www4.tpg.com.au/users/tps-seti/crater.html.

Penn State. "Global Warming Led to Atmospheric Hydrogen Sulfide and Permian Extinction." www.sciencedaily.com/releases/2005/02/050223130549.htm.

———. "Hydrogen Sulfide, Not Carbon Dioxide, May Have Caused Largest Mass Extinction." www.sciencedaily.com/releases/2003/11/031104063957.htm.

Raup, David M. *Extinction—Bad Genes or Bad Luck?* New York: W. W. Norton & Company, 1991.

Tudge, Colin. *Last Animals at the Zoo—How Mass Extinction Can Be Stopped*. Washington, D.C.: Island Press, 1991.

University Of Washington. "New Evidence Indicates Biggest Extinction Wasn't Caused by Asteroid or Comet." www.sciencedaily.com/releases/2005/01/050121 101514.htm.

———. "Ultra-low Oxygen Could Have Triggered Die-offs, Spurred Bird Breathing System." www.sciencedaily.com/releases/2003/10/031031062625.htm.

Ward, Peter D. *Gorgon: Paleontology, Obsession, and the Greatest Catastrophe in Earth's History.* New York: Penguin Group, 2004.

Whitehouse, David. "BBC News Online—Mystery Space Blast 'Solved.'" news.bbc.co.uk/1/hi/sci/tech/1628806.stm.

Wilson, Edward O. *The Future of Life.* New York: Alfred A. Knopf, 2002.

Further Exploration

BOOKS

Barrett, Paul. *National Geographic Dinosaurs*. Washington, DC: National Geographic Children's Books, 2001.

Elkins-Tanton, Linda. *The Solar System: Asteroids, Meteoroids, and Comets*. New York: Facts On File, 2006.

Erickson, John. *Lost Creatures of Earth: Mass Extinction in the History of Life*. New York: Facts On File, 2001.

Henderson, Doug. *Asteroid Impact*. New York: Dial Books for Young Readers, 2000.

Holmes, Thom and Laurie. *Great Dinosaur Expeditions and Discoveries: Adventures with the Fossil Hunters*. Englewood Cliffs, NJ: Enslow Publishers, 2003.

Jankins, Steve. *Life on Earth: The Story of Evolution*. Boston: Houghton Mifflin, 2002.

Lange, Ian. *Ice Age Mammals of North America*. Missoula, Mont.: Mountain Press Publishing Company, 2002.

Lawson, Kristan. *Darwin and Evolution for Kids: His Life and Ideas with 21 Activities*. Chicago: Chicago Review Press, 2003.

Simon, Seymour. *Comets, Meteors, and Asteroids*. New York: HarperCollins, 1998.

Sís, Peter. *The Tree of Life: Charles Darwin*. New York: Farrar, Straus and Giroux, 2003.

Tanaka, Shelley. *New Dinos: The Latest Finds! The Coolest Dinosaur Discoveries!* New York: Atheneum, 2003.

WEB SITES

www.pbs.org/wgbh/evolution/extinction/dinosaurs/index.html
The Public Broadcasting Station's site explains what killed the dinosaurs.

www.space.com/asteroids
Imaginova's site includes pages of images and the latest news articles about asteroids.

www.pbs.org/wgbh/evolution/library/03/index.html
The history of life—animated

homeschooling.gomilpitas.com/explore/fossils.htm
Fossils and fossil collecting

www.enchantedlearning.com/subjects/dinosaurs/extinction
Dinosaurs and extinction

www.EnchantedLearning.com/subjects/Geologictime.html
Geologic Time Scale

www.childrensmuseum.org/dinosphere/profiles/gorgo.html
Learn how a family of amateur paleontologists discovered a new dinosaur.

kids.msfc.nasa.gov/SolarSystem
Asteroids, meteorites, and other cool space stuff

www.stcms.si.edu/trial_teach/earth.htm
Earth in space, with lots of activities

www.EnchantedLearning.com/subjects/rainforest
www.endangeredspecie.com
Endangered species

www.EnchantedLearning.com/subjects/volcano
Volcanoes

www.worldwildlife.org
World Wildlife Federation

Index

Page numbers for illustrations are in *italic*

adaptations. *See* evolution
Age of Mammals, 27
Age of the Dinosaurs, 9–11, 19, 24, 26
Age of the Fishes, 19, *24*
Agricola, Georgius, *15*
air bubbles, 37–38
alligators, *48*
Alvarez, Luis and Walter, 28–29
archaeologists, 54
argon, 38
asteroids
    air bubbles and, 38
    Chicxulub, *10*
    craters and, *8*
    dust and, 31–32
    evidence for role of, 28–31
    iridium and, 37
    mass extinctions and, 19
    shocked quartz and, 30–31
    shooting stars and, *9*
    volcanos vs., 41–43
    Yucatán Peninsula and, 7–9
auks, *51*

background extinction, 56
basalt, *38*, 39, 40–41, *41*
biodiversity, 48, 61
birds, *40*, *49*, *51*, 55
body temperature, *50*
Boltysh Crater, 33
boundaries, *25*, 25
bubbles, 37–38

Cambrian Explosion of Life, 20, *22*
Canadian Rockies, *21*
carbon dioxide, 43–44
Cenozoic Era, *18*
chain reactions, 43–44
Chicxulub Crater, *10*, *32*, 32–33
circumstantial evidence, 30
climate, 19, 24
clouds, *7*, *35*
cockroaches, 53
competition, survival and, 48–49
conservation, *60*, 61

craters, 8, 32–34, 35
Cretaceous (K-T) mass extinction, *25*,
    25–27, 28–31, 33, *46*
Cretaceous Period, 19, 40

Darwin, Charles, *23*, 46
dating, rare elements and, 29
Deccan Traps, 40
Devonian mass extinction, 21–22
Devonian Period, 19, *24*
Dinosauria, *27*
dinosaurs
    birds and, *40*
    Chicxulub asteroid and, *10*
    Cretaceous (K-T) mass extinction and,
        26, *33*
    described, 9–11
    ecological niches and, 50
    oxygen and, *40*
    Triassic Period and, 24
diversity, ecosystems and, 58–59
dust, asteroids and, 31–32

eagles, *49*, *60*
ecological niches, 46–48, 50
ecosystems, importance of, 58–61
eggs, fossilized, 12, *13*
endangered species, *59*
energy, fossil fuels and, *56*
eras, defined, 17
erosion, fossils and, 13
evolution
    biodiversity and, 61
    Charles Darwin and, *23*
    humans and, 53–54
    mass extinctions and, 16–17
    natural selection and, 45–46
    paleontologists and, *12*
    survival and, 46–49
extinctions, human-caused, 56, 58,
    59–61

farming, humans and, 55–56
fish, 21–22
forests, 56–57, *59*
fossil fuels, *56*
fossils

About the Author

RANDI MEHLING is the author of several nonfiction books for young readers. She has written on a wide variety of health and science topics, including *Weather, and How It Works* and this book in Chelsea House's Scientific American series. Mehling has a passion for the natural world and our relationship with it. She is a published poet and essayist and holds a masters degree in public health.

Picture Credits